The '70s Colouring Book

First published 2016

The History Press
The Mill, Brimscombe Port
Stroud, Gloucestershire, GL5 2QG
www.thehistorypress.co.uk

Text © The History Press, 2016
Illustrations by Martin Latham © The History Press, 2016

British Library Cataloguing in Publication Data.
A catalogue record for this book is available from the British Library.

ISBN 978 0 7509 7048 8

Cover colouring by Lucy Hester.
Typesetting and origination by The History Press
Printed and bound in Great Britain by TJ International Ltd.

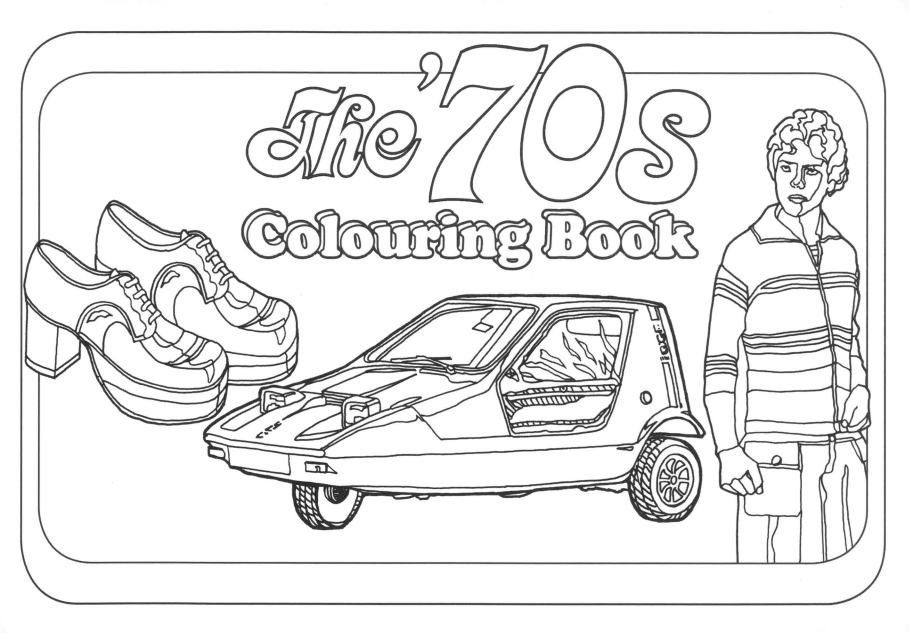

Chill out with this feel-good colouring book designed for everyone who loves the '70s.

Featuring 45 awesome illustrations, many from the Kays Heritage Group catalogue collection, you are sure to find a far-out picture waiting to be transformed with a splash of colour. From funky fashion and hip hairstyles to cool cars and groovy games, absorb yourself in the simple act of colouring to capture this incredible decade.

There are no rules – you can choose any combination of colours you like to bring these images to life.

With special thanks to Bernard Mills, Chairman of Kays Heritage Group, for permission to reproduce some of the images in this book from its catalogue collection.
www.kaysheritage.org.uk

Anita Harris models her collection of zingy
outfits for the fashion-conscious young
lady in the Kays Spring/Summer Catalogue
in 1971. (© Kays Heritage Group) ›

Action Man, the ultimate soldier. Accessories included a parachute, Operations Kit Bag, and Scorpion Tank with revolving turret. (© Kays Heritage Group) ▸

Ice lollies were particularly popular
during the heatwave of 1976. ›

The 'Canadiana' tableware range comprised
thirty pieces and was available from
the Kays Spring/Summer Catalogue in
1977. (© Kays Heritage Group) ▸

Ladies' lounge-style dresses featured flamboyant
colours and prints. (© Kays Heritage Group) ▸

The Ford Capri. ▸

Off to the pub? Stylish menswear featured cord suits, wide lapels and low-buttoned shirts with print-shoulder patches. (© Kays Heritage Group) ›

Platform shoes were the latest trend. (© Kays Heritage Group) ▸

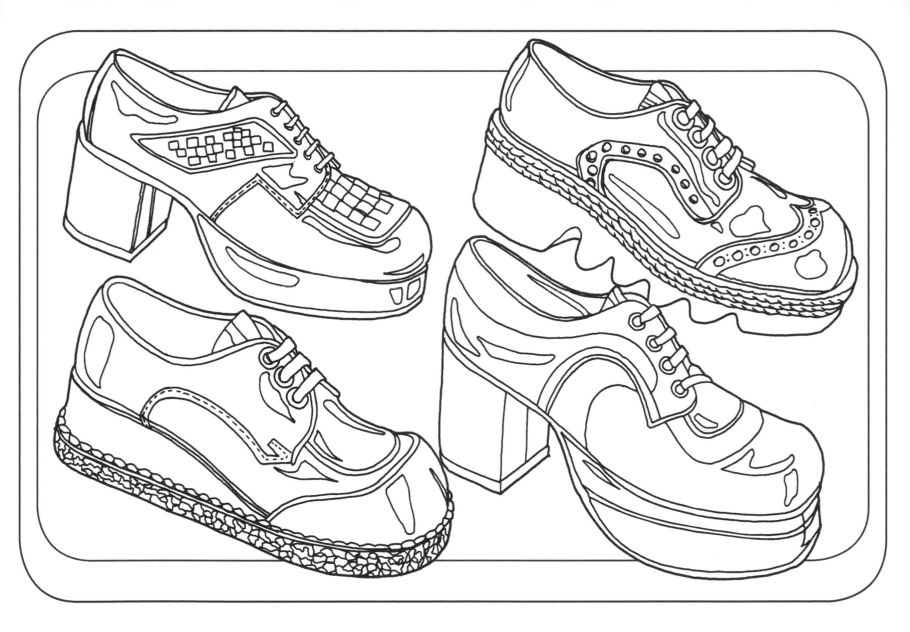

Fashion dresses modelled by actress and television presenter Anne Aston for the Kays Autumn/Winter Catalogue in 1972. (© Kays Heritage Group) ›

'70s glassware. ▷

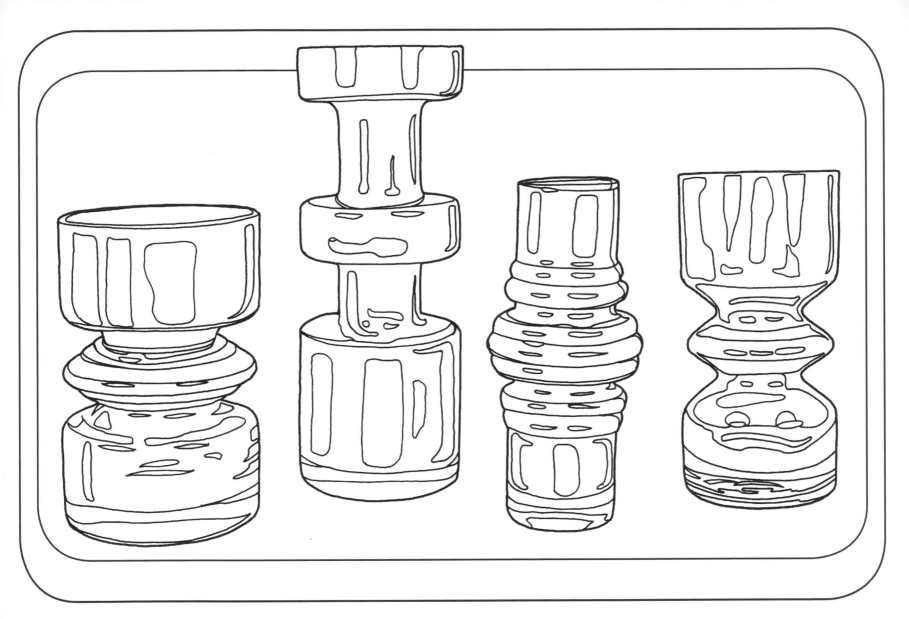

The 'Madrid' three-piece suite, available from the Kays Spring/Summer Catalogue in 1974. (© Kays Heritage Group) ▸

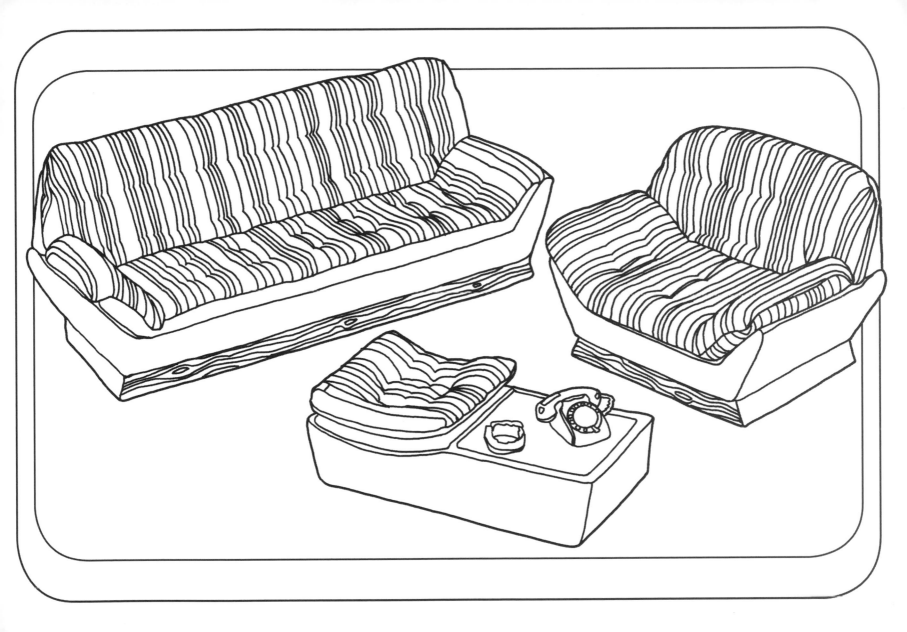

Sindy made her first appearance in
a Kays catalogue in 1963 and her last
in 1990. (© Kays Heritage Group) ▸

Punks wore their hair shaved, spiked, in a crew cut or Mohawk style. ▸

Simon – the classic electronic memory game. (© Kays Heritage Group) ▸

Before we all got into healthy eating we enjoyed coconut tobacco and lemonade shandy. ▸

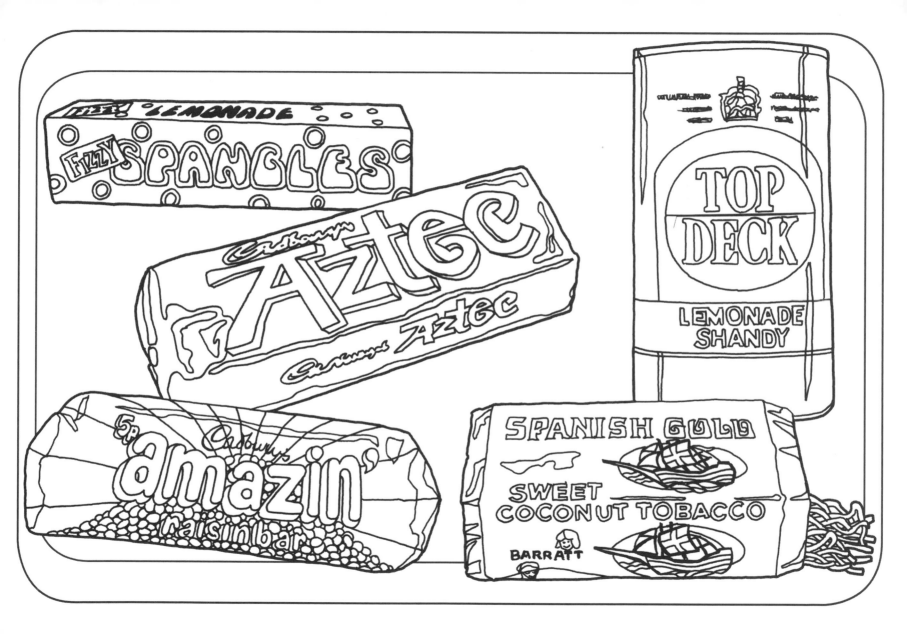

Teenage fashion. (© Kays Heritage Group) ▶

The ever popular *Doctor Who.*
(© Kays Heritage Group) ›

Mary Quant court shoes, with 2-inch heels. (© Kays Heritage Group) ▸

The Raleigh Chopper. ▸

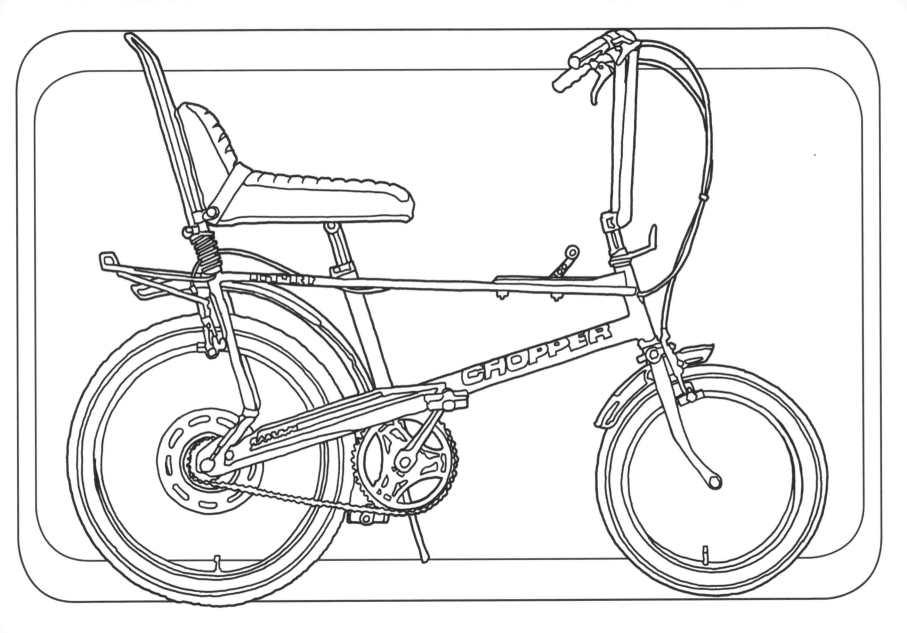

The Triumph TR7. ▸

Girls' fashion from the Kays Spring/Summer
Catalogue in 1977. (© Kays Heritage Group) ▸

Evel Knievel Stunt Cycle. (© Kays Heritage Group) ▸

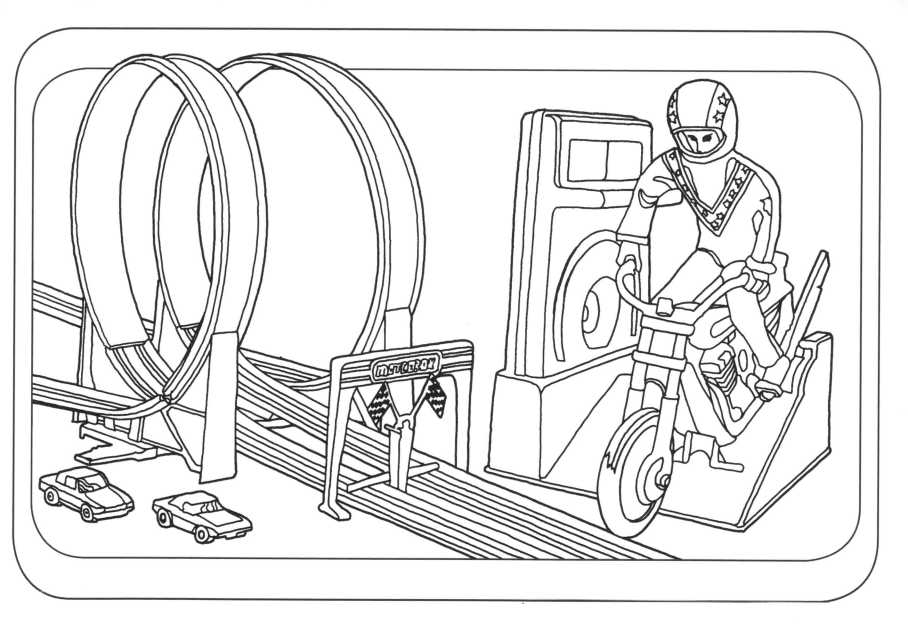

**Marc Bolan, David Bowie, Noddy Holder
and Rod Stewart – '70s musical icons.** ▸

Popular sweets from the '70s. ▸

Stylish outfits modelled by actress, singer and entertainer Anita Harris for the Kays Autumn/Winter Catalogue in 1972. (© Kays Heritage Group) ▸

Stockcar Smash Up. ▸

The Bond Bug – a two-seat, three-wheeled car. ▸

'70s vases. ▸

Bagpuss, the Clangers and The Wombles made for popular soft toys. ▸

**Ford Cortina – the UK's
best-selling car of the '70s.** ▸

**Swedish pop group ABBA
dominated the charts in the '70s.** ▸

Look-in, Bunty and *Jackie* were the
magazines to read for cool youngsters. ▸

Check jackets, polo-neck jumpers, flared trousers and anoraks were in vogue in the '70s. (© Kays Heritage Group) ▸

Polyester, acrylic and nylon were used
in the manufacture of many clothing
items. (© Kays Heritage Group) ▸

Lava lamps – the original mood lighting. ▸

Toys such as the UFO Shado's Space Fighter Interceptor, Space 1999 spacecraft, and Joe 90's flying car tied in with the decade's fascination with space exploration. ▸

**Roller skates and velour shirts were the ultimate
Saturday night outfit for young disco goers.** ›

The Bay City Rollers – 'the tartan
teen sensations from Edinburgh'. ›

Televisions, telephones and radios offered state-of-the-art design. ▸

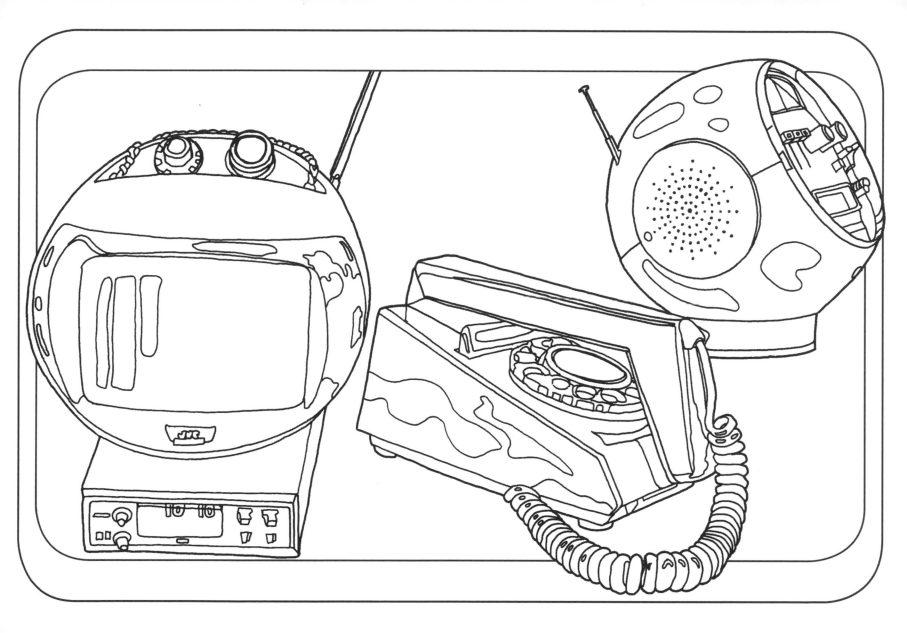

Three-piece suits – for the young man who appreciated fashionable tailoring. (© Kays Heritage Group) ▸

Matchbox, Hot Wheels and Dinky dominated Britain's toy car industry in the '70s. ▸

Even aprons, house coats and pinnies
were bright and fun in jumbo-print floral
designs. (© Kays Heritage Group) ▸

Popular toys included the Super Flight Deck, with a catapult action which launched the 'Phantom Jet', and the Walking Talking Robot, complete with four firing missiles. (© Kays Heritage Group) ▸

You can't beat a good sweater.
(© Kays Heritage Group) ▸

The ever-stylish Barbie and her British
counterpart, Sindy. (© Kays Heritage Group) ▸

Also from The History Press

A 1970s Childhood

From Glam Rock to Happy Days

DEREK TAIT